Forsaking All Others

A personal experience of recovery from adultery

Esther Anderson

Onwards and Upwards Publishers

Berkeley House, 11 Nightingale Crescent, Leatherhead,
Surrey, KT24 6PD.
www.onwardsandupwards.org

ISBN: 978-1-910197-90-5
Typeface: Sabon LT
Graphic design: LM Graphic Design

Endorsement

Esther's book is both personal and powerful. We would commend it to any couple seeking to rebuild their marriage following unfaithfulness. It does not make comfortable reading as Esther does not shy away from the hard realities of making tough decisions. But it will give hope and practical advice to any couple who are on a journey of restoration.

Nicky and Sila Lee
Founders of The Marriage Courses

Acknowledgements

To invaluable family and friends: Margaret, Jane Stanfield, Ian and Kathleen Wright, Lachlan and Marie Cameron, Jane Begg, Rachel Smith, James Duckworth, Dianne Harrison, Betty Kinghorn, Sarah Finegan, Ruth Jack, David and Hannah Sanderson, Elaine Stevenson, Thomas and Susanne Stephen, Julie Curran, Laura Stephen and Julie Fairley. *"A friend is someone who knows all about you and still loves you."* *(Elbert Hubbard)*

To my younger brothers David and Phil Stephen – for their broad shoulders.

To my patient work colleagues during the summer of 2012: Karen Allan (thanks for all the timely prayer promises), Louise Park, Val Beattie, Helen Martin, Colina Cockburn (thanks for being a great amateur psychologist), Lorraine Fields, Jackie Mathieson, Kathryn Hart, Steve Richardson (thanks for being a good man) and Elinor Pollock.

To Mark Fairley, Mim Emerton, Mary Alexander and Joanna Morrison for proof reading the manuscript and for all their helpful and meaningful comments.

To all at my outgoing church family during August 2012.

To all at my incoming church family at the time and beyond. They have no idea what their ongoing love and support has meant to me. Thank you for acceptance, accountability, for practical help, for wisdom and sound advice.

To John and Isobel Gibson – for solace in the first agonizing weeks.

To the 'Quiet Waters' Volunteer Counsellors, George and Sadie Abercrombie.

To all the staff at Onwards and Upwards Publishers, who worked to publish and promote this book, and especially to Luke Jeffery, Managing Director, who patiently guided me every step of the publishing way.

About the Author

Esther was born in 1967, the eldest of four, in a fishing town on the North East of Scotland. She qualified in Occupational Therapy at Queen Margaret College, Edinburgh in 1988 and has lived, married, worked in NHS and Social Work, and worshipped in the Central Belt of Scotland ever since.

Her hobbies include visiting and playing with her little nephews, reading, ancestry, worship music, photography and the West Coast of Scotland.

In memory of my Uncle Bruce

1947-2014

who lived for and died in Christ
"which is far better"

Dedication

I dedicate this book to Charlie,

my long-suffering, loving, kind,
forgiving husband.

You are very precious.

"We cannot change and learn if we will not learn to change."

Barry R Smiths

from the book 'First Person'

Contents

Author's Note

I mean no hurt, upset or offense to anyone by writing this book.

God rest us.
Rest the part of us that is tired.
Awaken the part of us that is asleep.
God awaken us and awake within us.[1]

Change [me] so that the energy of your forgiveness flows into bold and joyful action, into a humility which is not defeatism, into strength and confidence to be vulnerable.[2]

---

[1] *When I Talk to You: A Cartoonist Talks to God;* Michael Leunig; Andrews McMeel Publishing (2006); ISBN 970-0-7407-5696-2

[2] Confession 26 from *The Pattern of our Days, Liturgies and Resources for Worship;* Kathy Galloway; Wild Goose Publications (1996); ISBN 0-947988-76-9

Preface

I have primarily written this book for Christians, for those who believe that the Bible is the true Word of God. I say primarily, but I believe that all those who commit adultery will relate to the destruction, damage and despair that it causes, and will also be encouraged that there is hope in recovery and that with God, failure is not final.

One of the writers at 'Our Daily Bread' noted:

> *...like Paul, we don't need to parade our failures or to pretend they didn't happen.*[3]

On the one hand, this book does parade my failures, but on the other it is also an attempt to confront the fact that it did happen.

I have written as honestly as I can. On this topic, Rowan Williams states:

> *...if we are trying to write properly – that honest self-expression is the hardest thing in the world; it needs self-scrutiny and self–abandonment.*[4]

---

[3] *Our Daily Bread, Radio Bible Class;* David McCasland; 13th October 2013

[4] *Silence and Honey Cakes – The Wisdom of the Desert;* Rowan Williams; Lion Books (2003); ISBN 978-0-7459-5170-6

In essence this book is an expression of boldness mixed with vulnerability, and if truth be told, it has nearly not been written many times over. Thoughts that required scrutiny were:

"Do I add this in or keep it out?"

"Will this bring criticism or acclaim or both, and how will I deal with either?"

"What will the reaction be from those who know me best?"

"Am I doing this for the correct motives?"

In the end, I had to answer these questions honestly before pressing ahead.

In Pete Greig's book, 'God on Mute', he and his wife stated that they wished they had had a book which could have reached out to them at the time of their crisis. As there was none, Pete wrote 'God on Mute', which deals with a silent but present God in times of anguish and despair.

I wrote this book for similar reasons; there appears to be silence on this topic which needs to be filled. I hope that this is the book you hoped you would find during your time of great anguish and great despair.

I am well aware that I am not the first to fail in my adultery, nor will I be the last.

In my brokenness, this is my offering to reach others who are similarly broken.

Foreword

If others knew our innermost thoughts and desires, we would blush with shame. Yet in this book, Esther has let us inside not only her head but also her heart, for with breathtaking honesty she has revealed how she fell down the slippery slope that led to adultery. She has done this not as an attention-seeking exercise, but to help others save one of the most precious gifts God gives to married couples.

Using relevant biblical passages and referencing excellent Christian authors who have written extensively on the subject of marriage relationships, Esther takes us through her heartrending struggle with herself, her commitment to her husband, her faith and, in the end, her obedience to God.

I first met Esther and Charlie nineteen years ago when they lived in Stenhousemuir and worshipped at Larbert East for nearly three years before moving away. I knew Charlie's struggles with major health issues and how, as a couple, they faced these hurdles. This book shows that the marriage relationship needs constant work to deal with the issues that arise when we can take our loved one for granted.

If you are struggling with the temptation to follow a similar path to Esther or have already slid down the slope, read this book. If you know someone in that situation, persuade them to read this book. And if you are struggling to forgive someone who has torn you and your marriage apart, read this book. It might help you to find the 'you' God created you to be and restore you to the path of faithfulness.

Rev. Melville Crosthwaite BD., Dip. Ed., Dip. Min.
February 2016

Melville has been a Church of Scotland minister for thirty-two years, over twenty of which have been in Larbert East. Before that he was a teacher. Married to Irene, they have four children and, to date, two grandchildren. He is author of 'Team Tanzania', written following study leave as part of a Vine Trust Work Party to help children orphaned by Aids.

CHAPTER ONE

Introduction

I became a Christian by praying a simple, child-like prayer, asking Jesus into my heart and life at the age of seven in 1974. I was inspired by my younger sister, who had done the same thing a few months earlier. By the age of fifteen in 1982, I had re-committed my life to Jesus at a summer camp and from that moment on, as a young adult, I began taking my Christian life and witness seriously, including getting to know the Bible for myself and being baptized in water by full immersion.

As a young girl I became aware of three individuals caught in an adulterous situation within the church where I grew up. I remember the sense of horror and shame and the unspeakable nature of it. It was like a death and it was dealt with in great solemnity. I remember looking at the two women and one man as forever tainted.

Having now been similarly tainted, I sometimes long for the innocence of childhood and long to re-capture the sense of repulsion I felt towards sin. Once this repulsion is lost, it is almost impossible to regain.

Sin has a corrupting and contaminating effect. God's Word, however, and the truth of it, His people, His Spirit and His ways have a purifying effect, all of which can mature us into a new-found holiness. This gives me great hope and encouragement as I come to terms with the fact that I am a never-ending work-in-progress and that I am on, not so much a journey, but a life-long voyage.

When it comes to knowing what the Bible says about adultery, I cannot claim to have studied the Scriptures in their original languages. However, I understand in layman's terms what the Old Testament has to say about the topic and how Jesus, in the New Testament, handled the Pharisees when they brought a woman to Him who was caught in the very act of adultery. (A list of Bible references and a summary of Christian teaching can be found in the section entitled 'For Further Study' at the back of this book.)

However, it is so easy to disregard the rules.

At a silent retreat I went to, there was a rule: "Do not wear outdoor shoes beyond this point!" And I did – twice! I had perfectly understood the instruction but chose to ignore it.

Why are we like this?

And why are we like this with God's Word?

Why do we think that it is irrelevant or that it doesn't apply to us or, because we see someone else doing it and seemingly getting away with it, we think we will, too? How can we think that way when God is all-seeing?

As Philip Yancey states:

> *What I do <u>matters</u>. More, what I do matters to God, who created this world and set the rules we disregard at our peril.*[5]

Obedience / disobedience

On the one hand, there is God and life and blessing; on the other, Satan and death and curses. It would appear obvious to choose life, but clearly we still find the voice of the serpent highly seductive – ultimately to our own detriment and destruction. We should not follow the crowd in doing wrong. It may be a lonely road to follow Jesus but it is the right path to take.

We need to make the choice to absolutely revere God's Word and not be tempted to adjust it to correspond with our feelings or culture. We must always try to achieve clarity of truth amongst the confusion of life.

Essentially, we need to align our minds to what the Scriptures say, not align the Scriptures to our circumstances, or what we might want them to say. God's Word is to be obeyed whether we find it to be immediately to our liking or not. It is in becoming obedient to Him that we discover true freedom.

God does not ask us for our opinion, but he asks us for our wholehearted obedience – there is nothing else for it. My soul was condemned for years until the day I

---

[5] Taken from *Rumours of Another World* by Philip Yancey. Copyright © 2003 by Philip Yancey. Use by permission of Zondervan. *www.zondervan.com*

fully submitted to Him. It was only then, when I submitted to God's clear directives laid out in the Bible, that my soul had rest. I had to lay myself down, otherwise I was committing spiritual suicide.

Liberal Christians would accuse this way of interpreting the Bible as "party-line" thinking, but we cannot believe just bits of the Bible. People who do are in rebellion, I believe. Broadly speaking, we either have to believe all of it or we in effect believe none of it. The truth does not cease to exist just because it is ignored or manipulated or explained away.

CHAPTER TWO

My Story

2 Samuel 13:1-2
Amnon fell desperately in love with Tamar. He became so obsessed with her that he became ill.

1 Corinthians 10:13
No temptation has overtaken you but such is common to man.

I married my husband in 1991 when I was twenty-four and he was forty-four. He was a divorcee, and by marrying him I had been accused by some of being an adulterer as a result. He had been married to a woman who had also previously been married. For the purists, this would mean that his marriage to her was adulterous. However, she had committed adultery during her marriage to him, thus permitting my husband to remarry as the injured party. All of this happened whilst he was a non-believer, so all of his sins were forgiven at the point of salvation. But none of this was considered by our church elders at the time, who asked us to leave if we planned to pursue marriage as it would be seen by them as adulterous.

My husband had become a Christian at the age of forty-two and had had a Damascus Road type of conversion. Spiritually, he became my teacher, as his fresh, non-biased, non-denominational approach to the Scriptures taught me how much I had to unlearn before I could re-learn age-old truths. It was an exciting time being married to him as my spiritual life took off and under his encouragement I blossomed and developed a side of myself that had been hibernating – a creativity that had been stunted, cautious and afraid now blossomed. I even changed physically: I lost weight and grew more confident. People who had known me all of my life didn't recognize me after one year of marriage. My husband was, and still is, good for me.

Unfortunately, my husband has struggled with his health, and due to this I often find myself doing activities alone. He has long term health problems which have been ongoing for most of our married life. Although chronic in nature, occasionally there have been acute crises, with occurrences of life-threatening pneumonia which have resulted in intensive care admissions.

In October 2011, only seven months after he and I had co-founded a House Fellowship in our village, he contracted shingles in his left eye and forehead which was excruciatingly painful for him. Sadly, he never really managed to join us on a Sunday morning after that. I had been so happy during our months spent together and now, yet again, I was attending church on my own and I was devastated. The post-shingles neuralgic pain continues to plague him to the present, but it is accentuated and more problematic during the night. This, along with sleep apnoea and restless legs (his body is never at rest whilst he is asleep), leaves him constantly fatigued and often struggling emotionally to cope with and accept his limitations.

Very occasionally when I wouldn't be able to sleep, I would lie in the darkness and hear him struggling to breathe (or indeed stop breathing altogether). Every minute of every hour of every night, he was gasping for breath. It was too much. I would ask God in the dead of night to either heal him or take him. I suffered a lot of anguish listening to him suffer and often in these bleak moments I felt the light of joy and life dim and die within me. Then daylight would dawn and the pain would continue. I often wondered what God's purpose could be behind this tormented sleep pattern.

God has remained silent in this regard, but He has undoubtedly used my husband's illness to form and shape the person whom I've become – rather than battling with the questions, I have learned to accept the unfathomable. I find acceptance to be an incredible thing.

It was in September 2011, after twenty years of marriage and just a month before my husband contracted shingles, that I met the man whom I would later commit adultery with. This man's best friend had recently died and we became good friends after spending time together whilst practicing for a worship event. It was there we found a shared love of playing our instruments and singing God's praises.

He was full of life and creativity. He was especially generous with his time, talents, and finances. We found

21

it easy to talk to each other openly and honestly, and when I became aware that we were tuning into each other's emotions and that we had mutually connected and bonded in every possible way, I asked to speak with him after a church service one evening in April.

Falling in love is dreadfully powerful, and a totally unwelcome event to occur when you are already married.

I admitted to him then that this was not the first time I had found myself in this situation and that I didn't want to repeat it as it had nearly destroyed me. At first he was in disbelief, but two months later he declared that he, similarly, had fallen in love with me.

We discussed the boundaries that would be required to protect us from our own feelings – the first being no touching or hugging.

Whilst I did not resent my husband, at times I resented the effects that his ill-health had on our lives together. While I was very happy to be with him and care for him, I became restless. I would never be with him in the evenings and then I would feel guilty and go to the other extreme of never going out. It was difficult to maintain a balance between caring for my husband and trying to find fulfilment for my own spiritual and physical needs.

Previously, I had volunteered as a telephone counsellor with Crossline and at the same time volunteered with Prison Fellowship, but after a couple of years I had given both up. I had led at twelve Alpha groups over twelve years, but again I had given up the position, feeling that I was at times 'running on dry'. I had tried hill-walking for some years, even walking the hills every Sunday instead of attending a church fellowship, but that didn't feel right.

I felt resigned to a life of compromise. This was not the life I had imagined, nor was it how I thought it was meant to be. I can recall what I expected my future to be like when I was young and single: I expected to remain single and be pious, a missionary maybe, away from the suffocating atmosphere of 80s materialistic Britain.

At the time when I was bonding with my new male friend, my husband and I were discussing living separately. We had just moved house and he wanted to move again and, frankly, I didn't want to. We had no children. My new friend was forty-eight, had been married for eighteen years with two sons still living at home, aged seventeen and fifteen. After a couple of months of attending our House Fellowship together with their younger son, he and his wife had had a candid discussion about faith and his wife concluded that she no longer believed the Bible or its message. They also had a frank discussion about their marriage and decided to separate; he took up temporary residence in his own accommodation.

From then on, each of the boundaries that we had agreed upon were slowly crossed, one by one; first holding hands, next kissing. We often grabbed a few moments together after work in a car park or lay-by. This escalation of intimacy eventually resulted in us committing adultery several times during a four-week period in his new accommodation.

I was still attending my former church. As I travelled the distance from the new house to the church, I passed the other man's new accommodation. On the first

occasion that we committed adultery, I had popped in to
see him on my way home to give him some money I owed
him.

I knew having sex with this man was wrong. Why,
then, did I do it? Why would I go against the very
morality I believed in? Why would I compromise myself?

Why indeed.

I have found no satisfactory answer other than it was
completely selfish and reckless. I was certainly playing
with fire. In those short, brief moments of abandonment,
the only thing that mattered was satisfying myself. Any
thoughts of God, spouse or others were compartment-
alized, blocked off and shut down.

What was I thinking?

One quote seemed to sum it up:

> *We don't run away from our values, we drift
> away and wake up in places we never meant
> to. Sin is subtle; it lures you into thinking you
> have it all together, then one day you discover
> you're in over your head.*[6]

I think it is possible to be totally deceived by one's
own emotions – emotions that are so powerful at the
time that they override logic, faith and sense. They are
like an all-consuming tsunami, sweeping you up and
propelling you along in a fast and destructive momentum
that is almost impossible to avoid once it strikes.

The mind is also incredibly deceitful. It can convince
you that wrong is right and right is wrong; or, at least,

---

[6] John Blumberg

24

that the wrong that you do in secret will have no consequences.

And at first, there appeared to be no immediate consequences to my adultery. However, I knew that what I was doing was morally wrong and it gradually took its toll. My agonizing turmoil had begun at this point.

I loved my husband, but there was no doubting that I also loved this man and that the feeling was mutual. He told me that he had never loved so completely, nor been so completely loved. Influenced by the sheer force and power of 'eros' and having newly fallen in love, some people make decisions at this point to devastate their partners and leave them and follow their desires.

Certainly I had lost my heart to someone other than my spouse. My lover had come between me and my first love, becoming a huge distraction and an idol. This was, of course, as true for him as it was for me.

I left home for three nights to consider my options and they were the toughest days of my life.

I actually knew on the first day that I wanted to return to my husband. That first night I had stayed with a friend. The second night I spent with the other man. By the middle of the next day I told him I was planning to return to my husband. He and another friend persuaded me to stay one more night to give myself more time to think, but I had already made up my mind.

Essentially I had two choices. I felt strongly that I should do God's Will and not follow my own selfish will; what I had done was already selfish enough. Either way, there were painful consequences to face. Ray Lawrence explains the nature of selfish desires well:

> *Even the best people have to wrestle with this – we have all permitted ourselves to be seduced by the philosophy of 'me first' where we think about ourselves, talk about ourselves, do our own thing, promote our own fancies and feather our own nests – and we think [that this] will make us happy. In fact they do no such thing.*[7]

It is impossible to be at peace with sin and God at the same time. It is imperative to have a clear conscience before Him; this cannot be underestimated, as Timothy wrote:

1 Timothy 1:19
...by rejecting conscience, certain persons have suffered shipwreck in the faith.

Where there is immorality there is godlessness and I wanted to avoid this.

It was time to make right all the wrongs. I knew that making the right decision wouldn't instantly change my feelings but that eventually my feelings would catch up with my decision. This, ultimately, proved to be the case. As Dr James Dobson said, in 'Love Must Be Tough':

> *...nothing can seem so fixed but can change so rapidly as human emotions.*

It was time to confess.

---

[7] *The Choice: God First, or Me First?;* Ray Lawrence; The Plain Truth (Spring-Summer 2013)

CHAPTER THREE

Confession

Confession is not telling God how we have sinned. He already knows. Confession is simply agreeing with God that our acts were wrong ... How can God heal what we deny? ... How can God grant us pardon when we won't admit our guilt? ... What does guilt imply if not that we know right from wrong ... [and have] a healthy regret for telling God one thing and doing another.[8]

1 John 1:9
If we confess our sins, He is faithful and just and will forgive us our sins and purify us from all unrighteousness.

It was the 10th of September, 2012. This was the day I confessed my adultery to my husband. I remember exactly where we were and precisely what we were doing when he asked me if there was someone else. We were in

---

[8] Taken from *A Gentle Thunder* by Max Lucado. Copyright © 2003 by Max Lucado. Used by permission of Thomas Nelson. *www.thomasnelson.com.*

the car, turning into our driveway having been out for the day. I could have lied but this was my opportunity to come clean.

It was terrifying. I had no idea how my husband would react or whether he would want to stay together. All I knew was that I wanted us to remain a couple.

At the point of confession there is huge fear, deep humiliation, a humbling, but also great relief. However, as any soldier knows, when external war ends, the internal battle is often about to begin.

Confession to God

Although you may keep secrets from people, there is nothing done on earth which God does not see. So I knew that He knew of my sin. I told Him that I was sorry. I felt that I had disappointed Him. I knew that this was not the way He wanted me to live. I asked Him to help me solve the mess I was in. I asked for His forgiveness and knew that I had received it. I knew that my relationship with God had not prevented me from doing what was defiling in His eyes, so my relationship with Him alone was not enough to break my pattern of sin. I had to stop the secretiveness and confess it to others.

Confession to others

As well as confessing to my husband, I also confessed to friends and family. I made a special trip to see my parents and spent an afternoon with them baring my soul. I remember that my mother rightly said that if a couple are to split up, it should never be the believer that leaves (see 1 Corinthians 7:15). This comment was made in relation to the fact that the other man, a believer, had left his wife, a non-believer.

I remember that my father said nothing except to say that he thought I looked too thin and needed to put on weight.

I told my brothers. One was on an oil rig and the other lives in the USA so we communicated with each other across time zones by live-messaging on Facebook.

I separately told perhaps twenty friends (some mutual to me and my lover) over the months and each of them agreed to support and pray for all of us.

At first I spoke of nothing else. Each development, each struggle, each problem, each emotion was spoken out, shared and discussed, more often than not accompanied with tears.

Confession to the church

The fellowship I attend had twenty-one members at the time, and during early 2013 we were given the option of sharing testimony together. I was scared but decided to face my fears and make a public confession whilst thirteen of our members were present, some of whom knew both me and my lover.

My testimony was this: "Should any of you struggle, don't keep it a secret, because this is the way that Satan isolates you in your shame. Share it with someone. Your struggle may not be mine, nor mine yours, but my prayer is that my failure can be my ministry."

It is easy to provide a false reputation of yourself, or to portray an image that all is well when it is not. In an attempt to stop myself from doing this, I asked one of our mutual friends if I could confide in her whatever I was feeling. This way, she and her husband could pray for us. This type of accountability has been invaluable, to the point of being painfully so; there have been times I have had to confess to selfishness, double-mindedness, stupidity and shameful things I have done in secret. However, when you are accountable to someone, it stops the pretence and the secretiveness from returning. It meant I could be truthful and it was a huge relief.

The next step for me was repentance (though it does not automatically follow; it has to be a choice – I know of people who have confessed but not repented).

Writing about repentance, Max Lucado states:

> *Repentance is the decision to turn from selfish desires and seek God ... You look at the love of God and can't believe He's loved you like he has and this realization motivates you to change your life. That is the nature of repentance.*[9]

---

[9] *Walking with the Saviour;* Max Lucado; Tyndale House Publishers (1996); ISBN 978-0-8423-7930-4

CHAPTER FOUR

Consequences

Psalm 31:7:
...you care about the anguish of my soul.

As a result of our sin, there were colossal consequences for all four of us. In committing adultery, I sinned against God, my own body, my husband, the other man and the other man's wife.

Consequences for my husband

My husband's immediate reaction was to phone the other man and warn him off. During the first few hours, he soothed me as I sobbed. He wanted me to be able to tell him everything that had happened, just as I would talk to my best friend. I determined that if he asked me any question, I would answer them honestly. I often felt uncomfortable discussing my affair, but given that I had been in the wrong, I was resolved to do whatever it took to make it right. These conversations, which took place over many months, always left me feeling terribly low as I spoke about what had been done in secret.

My husband didn't use harsh words against me, but one day five months after my initial confession he told me that I had been selfish and had no respect nor loyalty towards him – and he was right. He said that he didn't want to rule out separation or divorce (which he was entitled to do, given divorce is permitted on the grounds of adultery), and we agreed to see a Christian counsellor after that conversation.

He felt insecure and it would take a long time to build up his trust in me again.

Consequences for the other man's wife

Though claiming to not be a Christian, I found that the reaction of the other man's wife was very Christ-like.

She and I had known each other for a few months and we had liked each other.

When her husband left her, she told me that she was shocked, upset and angry. She said that she wanted things to go back to the way they were, but she realized that this would not be fair on him due to the way their marriage had been.

On confession of the adultery committed a month after their separation, he asked her if she wanted a divorce on the grounds of adultery and she declined.

We have bumped into each other twice since the affair, and on the second occasion I told her how deeply sorry I was for what I had done and asked for her forgiveness. She was gracious enough to say she held nothing against her husband or me and that life was too short for such attitudes. I certainly did not deserve this sort of favour, but I genuinely believe I have received her forgiveness. I believe she is an exceptional woman.

Much later, she told someone else that the whole experience had put her off the church. I take responsibility for my actions and the terrible damage they caused the witness of the church. There is no way to repair this damage other than to make it my prayer that all concerned can be restored and that she can come to know Jesus, the only Perfect One.[10] I also pray this for all of you reading.

Consequences for the other man himself

Put simply, this man's heart was broken and he experienced all of the reactions of grief: denial, anger, bargaining, depression and acceptance – not in a neat orderly way but backwards and forwards and round in circles.

He was wounded, and during the first three months after I had decided to return to my husband, he was often unable to work and at times he was unable to keep food down or sleep.

He had several mini mental health breakdowns; on one occasion he required professional input, and on a few occasions, during which times he was suicidal, he would disappear. He felt desolate. He felt that I had rejected and abandoned him. He had a crisis of faith. For a time, he stopped playing his guitar which had been his constant companion and inspiration since he had been a teenager.

---

[10] I am delighted to report that, having moved village, she is currently involved in the church there.

I feared for him. I was the cause of his pain – and this tormented me – but I was very firm about the fact that I could not be responsible for his actions or behaviour. I could not go to him to relieve his pain; God told me, "Leave him to me." I realized in my heart that I was not the cure for his problems, nor had I caused all of them. I could not be his rock or his saviour as I felt he wanted me to be.

He would swing from understanding what I was doing and why to speaking words of self-pity and hurt. He criticised me for staying with a chronically ill husband, saying that I had a passion for sympathy and that I revelled in my misery. He told me that my marriage was a lie and that the only person I loved was myself. He said he wasn't quite sure if I was sociopathic, insincere or just afraid.

These words were hard to hear and although I could choose not to take them on board, they had been said and their effects lingered for many days (and still do).

His GP prescribed exercise as a means of reducing stress and this, coupled with acquiring a dog and having the support of friends, has, I believe, saved his life.

He and his wife were divorced on the 6th of June, 2013, a few months after his father died. He was to see 2012-2013 as 'the year that the worm turned'.

Consequences for me

Immediately after I confessed, my secret inner turmoil came to the surface and became unspeakable anguish which was felt, to some extent, every day for months. It was a brutal, unbearably bleak time as I battled with selfish temptations. It was the worst mental suffering I had experienced in a very long time.

I may have resolved to stay with my husband because I loved him, because it was the right thing to do and it was unthinkable and wrong to leave him, but my flesh rebelled. The selfish influences that are buried deep within us will fight when we try to do the right thing. Knowing and doing what was right didn't stop the emotional roller-coaster. I believed at times that my husband would be better off living without me. I believed that it was because of my sin that he was not being healed. I also missed the other man and longed for him terribly at times. I mourned his loss like one would mourn for someone who had died a violent death.

I knew I was in a spiritual war. Being spiritual is counter-cultural and counter-natural. I knew that.

At times of pain and crisis, there is no doubt that faith is tested. But at the same time, faith is activated, and the lessons that we learn in the settled times become the building blocks to handle the crisis. Rather than let faith crumble, faith should strengthen, providing the rock and the steadiness needed when feelings are volatile, shaky and vulnerable.

I concluded that one path would include pain in sin but the other would be pain in obedience.

I lost a stone in weight. I came down with cystitis during the first week. My muscles seized up, and I experienced severe cramps in my legs and toes and had an IBS flare up. Eventually I was persuaded to visit my G.P. and was placed on a twenty-four-hour heart monitor. It transpired that my heart rate was constantly high with sheer adrenaline brought about by a great deal of fear and distress.

I was afraid of causing my husband further hurt. I was afraid that I had damaged our marriage too much. I was afraid for my own physical and mental health. I was afraid that the other man would kill himself. I was afraid that it would not end well for any of us.

I visibly aged during this time.

Someone said that they thought I was with the wrong man and that God didn't mean for any of us to be in servitude. Someone else said that I had been the devil's honey-pot that the other man had fallen into. I took one day off sick from work and I lay on the couch while my heart pounded for hours.

I hauled my body out of bed most days to go to work as I knew it was important not to spend sixteen hours per day thinking about it. Going to work gave my mind the respite and distraction it needed and helped to force me to think and focus on other issues and, more importantly, on other people.

As I tackled one problem, however, another one would appear to take its place. It was relentless and at times it was such a wearing, agitating force that I simply wanted to run away from everyone and everything. It seemed easier not to take responsibility than to always have to face the day with feelings of heaviness, dread and regret.

I took solace, however, from realising that I had moved from darkness to light, and that I had made the right decision to stay in my marriage.

Like Paul Nicholson wrote in 'Growing into Silence':

> *There are times when I simply know what it*
> *is I should do, without any doubt entering in.*
> *I may or may not be able to give convincing*
> *reasons for my choice but I could not take*
> *another path and be true to myself.*[11]

More subtly, I was in danger of developing an air of superiority, seeing myself as having coped with the self-inflicted stress better than the other man had done.

Just as we wait for the long, dark, bleak days of winter to pass into spring, so recovery can't be rushed or forced. But time does pass and things do ease and although, like the weather, recovery cannot always be predicted, life does settle down.

Despite this, I continue to live with the consequences of what I have done. It is harassing, intrusive, all pervasive and ultimately inescapable. It will be with me for the rest of my life.

Read and be warned.

---

[11] *Growing into Silence;* Paul Nicholson SJ; Way Books (2011); ISBN 978-0904717-34-1

CHAPTER FIVE

Dealing with Lies and Deceit

Jeremiah 17:9 (NIV)
The heart is deceitful above all things and beyond cure. Who can understand it?

I have to confess that this has been the hardest chapter to write, given that it exposes my true heart and the way it hardened and softened and struggled over the months.

> *I am more sinful than I ever imagined – and also more loved by God ... [However,] the moment I am most aware of my own inadequacy, at that moment I am probably closest to God.[12]*

During counselling in March 2013, it was agreed that if I was concentrating on rebuilding the relationship with my husband, there must not be any communication with the other man.

---

[12] Taken from *Rumours of Another World* by Philip Yancey. Copyright © 2003 by Philip Yancey. Use by permission of Zondervan. *www.zondervan.com*

I found letting go of our communication the thing I struggled with the most. At times I needed decisive words from important people to be jolted from the contradictions in my behaviour.

Lack of communication has to be the greatest gift that you can give to each other. It has to be done out of respect and loyalty for the partner you are returning to. It is a must. For the other person, it may feel cruel, but it is cruel to be kind. They are not able to move on if communication continues.

As long as there is communication, there are three people in the marriage. You cannot have it both ways. If you want your marriage, you cannot be in touch with the other person. If you want communication with the other person, you cannot have your marriage.

There are a multitude of ways to communicate in this technological age, so there are many things you have to tackle to ensure communication is stopped.

It is imperative to learn to let communication go.

Mobile phones

I changed my private mobile number right away, but it took nineteen months before I changed my work mobile number.

Email

I deleted the other man's address from my private email address book right away, but it took fourteen months to block him from using my work email address. In the end, I had to change my work email address nineteen months later, at the same time as changing my work mobile number, both of which were inconvenient and costly to my employer.

Facebook

I immediately removed him from Facebook as a friend, but for a while I failed to realize that while my page was public he could still see my posts. After discovering this, I made my site private for a few months then I made it public again before finally making it private again.

Private messages could still be sent and I could still see his comments, and he mine, on mutual friends' pages. I then made a move to take off our eleven mutual friends.

In the end, I blocked him; I had not known that I could do this and my youngest brother helped me with it fourteen months later.

It all took time. If I had to do it all over again, knowing what I know now, I would advocate blocking the person right away.

Smartphone

I bought my first smartphone in March 2014 and it took me a couple of months to realize that photos taken with the phone which were posted onto Facebook were made public unless I specifically made them private. This meant he could still see public items if he was signed in as another user.

So I made my phone photos private, too, but it took me a couple more months to finally make that change because I was still struggling with wanting him to see certain aspects of my life, even if it was just a holiday picture.

Other communications

Despite modern communications, there are always the old ways of keeping in touch, like writing letters or posting cards. There are always ways to see each other (or avoid each other) if you know one another's routines. All these things have to be tackled if they persist.

I stopped shopping at the supermarket where I knew he tended to shop and I began buying groceries online. At work I parked in a different car-park to usual and I even moved house. Sometimes it can become necessary to change job or to move out of the area completely so that there is no way of bumping into each other, even by accident.

Rebuilding your life is a minefield, but when you want to flee temptation, why would you want to leave a forwarding address?

CHAPTER SIX

Recovery

2 Samuel 14:14
*But God does not just sweep life away;
instead, he devises ways to bring us back
when we have been separated from him.*

I prefer to use the word "recovery" rather than "healing". After all, if you drop a clay pot and it shatters or cracks, can it ever be the same again? Even when glued back together, while it can become functional again, it still bears the outward and inner scars.

The Japanese had a novel way of fixing a cracked pot: they mended it using gold; thus, the original non-valuable everyday item became infinitely more valuable. This helps me to see my brokenness quite differently. I might not be useless after all. I just might be valuable, even with all my visible flaws.

In this chapter I will list the things that worked towards my inner recovery – work that I had to do for myself, and work that all the support from friends and family could never have achieved for me.

Prayer

Sometimes the only prayer I could manage to utter, such was my distress, was simply, "Help me, help me." I desperately wanted my marriage to survive and to come out of the other end stronger. I desperately wanted wisdom to know how to navigate each day. I prayed desperate prayers for my husband, for the other man's wife and for him. I needed to make sense of the experience and what I could learn from it. I wanted to grow. I wanted to become more like Jesus and I simply prayed for all of these things.

Weeping

I do believe that the ability to weep is a safety valve. Some people perhaps drink (more) alcohol during tough times as a means of helping them to cope. Some people perhaps take prescribed chemical medication or illegal drugs. Some perhaps over-eat or can't manage to eat at all. Some manage to talk whilst others clam up. Some need professional input whereas others do not. We all have different coping mechanisms.

As a person who doesn't drink alcohol at all, didn't get offered (or want) prescribed chemical medication (I did take a supplement bought from a Health Food Shop), and couldn't really eat properly due to nausea, I feel that my ability to weep and weep uncontrollably was a very healthy and healing experience (there is the word healing, after all!)

Bible reading

I believe that the discipline of daily Bible reading also aided my stability. I have a Chronological Bible in the New Living Translation and for three years I have read it every day without fail. I found that the words "abandoned" and "restore" stood out for me during the first year, and I began to underline them every time I came across them. For obvious reasons, in the second year the word "faithful" stood out. It the third year it was the words "obey" and "wisdom". I realize that throughout this process God has been asking for my total obedience to Him as a sign that He is my 'everything' and that He is enough.

And I have found that He is.

Nothing is essential but God.

He has created us to be in relationship with Him and with each other, and without either we are incomplete.

No matter what my day had been like or what voices I had been listening to during the day, I found that by reading my bible in the evening, I could once again "renew my mind" and realign my thoughts to scriptural truths and to what I knew was right despite the tug of war in my emotions.

Keeping a journal

I highly recommend writing things down. The confusion gets pushed away and the truth of it stands stark and naked – not always a comfortable matter.

I kept a notebook handy at all times so that I could write down occurrences, quotes, lines of songs, prayers, Bible verses, poems, insights, thoughts and feelings, and put them in date order. If I had any inspiration at all, whilst driving or showering or waking up in the morning, I would reach for my notebook and scribble it down.

It really helped to get jumbled and confusing thoughts out of my head and onto paper. I found it therapeutic and began to make sense of thoughts and feelings so I could begin to understand them. It helped me to see a pattern emerging and also helped to chart my progress.

It served to correct false memories and selective amnesia whilst writing this book. It is remarkable how much can be forgotten or wrongly recalled with the passing of time. My journal entries are in essence how this book was birthed.

Accountability

As mentioned earlier, I chose to be accountable to a female friend at church – someone who was also a friend of my lover. There were two other people that I chose to keep up to date with events as they happened whether they showed me in good light or not.

Regarding lies, the only way to peace is through truth. When asked a question, tell the truth. Don't build lies back into your life after you have done the initial groundwork of confessing. Try to be up to date with your spouse and resist the temptation to grow secretive and deceitful again, even if it is only about your emotions.

Overall, I now "strive always to keep my conscience clear before God and man"[13]. This is my ultimate goal.

Reading

I was terrified of becoming apathetic, of sinking and lacking the inner will to rise. I chose to read, read, read – mainly Christian books about marriage.

I learned that marriage is a covenant relationship. It represents the relationship between Christ and His church. No other relationship is meant to be lifelong – not the one with your children, or the one with your parents, only the one with your marriage partner.

The vows that we took so solemnly and yet so joyfully on the day of our marriage were symbolically entering us into an unbreakable covenant relationship and yet, it would seem, our commitment is so shallow when put to the test.

I continue to read, to keeping learning, to keep growing and to keep understanding. I never want to become complacent.

Books can challenge, encourage and enlighten, and they were a lifeline for me.

I have notebooks full of quotes from all of the books that I read; each one of them contributed to my recovery.

Songs

As a Christian musician, I survive and thrive whilst listening to worship music. Worship songs have an ability not only to interest me with a catchy tune, but,

---

[13] Acts 24:16 (NIV)

more importantly, the words sung (often pure Scripture) are able to penetrate my mind and feed my soul.

All types of music touch my soul, but I tend to avoid listening to love songs as I don't find them helpful in nurturing healthy emotions.

This song by Greg de Blieck, a Scottish songwriter, helped to sum up my thoughts whilst on an island trip:

> *This is a holy place*
> *How can I be here, how can I show my face?*
> *For what do I deserve?*
> *No more than judgment and disgrace*
>
> *How can I enter Your presence lightly*
> *Forgetting all You've done,*
> *   forgetting all You've done?*
> *Let me remember Your sacrifice*
> *And the price at which this freedom was won*
>
> *I am a sinner yet*
> *How deeply I've wounded, how shallow my regret*
> *And though I don't deserve*
> *Your blood has cancelled out my debt*
>
> *O Spirit now begin,*
> *Come sanctify me, and break this heart of sin*
> *And let my life become*
> *A place that Christ might enter in.*[14]

---

[14] *This is a Holy Place;* Greg de Blieck; from *New Scottish Hymns;* New Scottish Arts (2012)

Counselling

Whilst I am a talker, my husband is not.

Our counsellors told us that a lot of couples who come to them often want different things. Perhaps one wants to leave and the other wants to stay. In our case, we had done a lot of talking prior to going (six months of talking, in fact) and had completed a lot of the hard work beforehand. Both of us wanted the same thing – to remain in our marriage – and I felt that the greatest benefit of counselling was that it helped my husband open up to another man.

We had one session together at the beginning with both counsellors present. The aim of this session was for them to get to know us and observe our interaction together. We then had two separate sessions where I met with the female counsellor and my husband met with the male counsellor. Our final session was all together.

In total, we undertook four sessions, each between sixty and ninety minutes long.

We signed a counselling contract and both of us had a worksheet prepared for us which had practical tips. Some examples are:

- Talk to each other openly and honestly.
- Identify problems and disappointments in your marriage.
- Work towards forgiveness and building trust.
- Avoid being the cause of your spouse's unhappiness.
- Meet your spouse's emotional needs – identify what those needs are.

- Plan some date times and give undivided attention during that time.
- Have honesty – allow access to each other's mobile phones, etc.
- Account for my time.
- Avoid any contact with the other person.

The male counsellor asked my husband how long he was willing to work on our marriage and he said two years.

At the two-year point, my husband told me that he was proud of me. How could he be proud of me? A man that I had hurt being proud of the one who had hurt him? How could this be?

I know that he had witnessed my efforts to make things right. He had witnessed the battle that I had had with myself. But ultimately I think he was proud of the fact that I had put God's Will before my own and that I was putting my spiritual life before my self-life.

I am pleased to say that at the time of writing we are still together, and I think that this is worth celebrating. We hope to renew our vows in August 2016 for our 25th wedding anniversary, and our vows will include the line "forsaking all others".

Special Events

One week after confessing, I visited Lindisfarne with two friends. My heart was in agony and I had cystitis but this "thin place"[15] was good for my soul. I visited Durham a year later to view the actual Lindisfarne gospels and was thrilled to have seen them.

I attended a women's Clan conference in Oban during the spring of 2013. The conference was where I allowed time for my Maker to speak to me and rebuke me. This was where I dealt with the guilt of having committed adultery and the depression associated with the failed hope of remaining faithful in my marriage. It was there that I gave myself permission to grieve, to feel the sadness of it all and to lament and cry once again. It was where there was encouragement to "keep walking through" and where I prayed for help to love God all of my days, in all of my ways, with all of my heart, all of my soul, all of my mind and with all of my strength.[16]

A friend came to me at the end of the evening session and said that she felt that God would reward me for my faithfulness (for being trustworthy, loyal, utterly reliable, true to my word and constant). I was completely overwhelmed as I felt anything but faithful.

I attended a Lydia Prayer Event in East Calder during early summer 2013 at a friend's parents' home. Here, I submitted to His ways – His higher ways. I knew that in His presence there is peace and rest and joy and life. I knew that by submitting, I had peace of mind, life in the Spirit and rest for my soul. I was exhorted to "hold on

[15] A "thin place" is a physical location but one that feels spiritual – where the connection to God and His presence is easily made and felt.

[16] See Judges 6:14

tightly without wavering"[17], fully trusting Him because God can be trusted.

I was very encouraged.

I attended a Silent Retreat during autumn 2013, two days after moving house. That was where I began putting this book together. Being silent was easy. Being still was not.

I learned to slow my thinking, my eating, my walking and my breathing.

We were discouraged from bringing a book to the retreat. Our mobiles and laptops were left in the car.

Travelling to the retreat, I had listened to the 2009 song 'Beautiful Things' by Michael and Lisa Gungor.[18] I learned that there is hope for recovery and that beauty is often birthed in a struggle.

I stood at the wooden cross in the grounds and wept when I spotted the nails. I walked around it, silently 'singing' the hymn 'When I Survey the Wondrous Cross'.

I found a picture in the foyer by Oliver Main – the I IF I portrait, shaped as a cross and made from shattered pale green sea glass foraged from the shore. What it spoke to me of was that our shattered lives can be made whole by the cross.

I reflected whilst lying prostrate in the prayer room with the Sudan cross on the wall that when we are cold, God is our warmth. When we are in darkness, He is our light. When we are dry, He is our rain and refreshment.

---

[17] Hebrews 10:23

[18] You can read the lyrics online at
www.metrolyrics.com/beautiful-things-lyrics-gungor.html

Mary Oliver's poem 'The Journey' was read to us as a group at the end of our silence.[19]

I began to be attracted to the rhythm of life of the Early Desert Fathers who lived a life in community. The simplicity of their way of living appealed to me. Their communities offered hospitality and their vows included those of chastity, obedience and poverty (poverty not being defined as being without money but rather as being without things we would like to have). They lived simply, holding possessions loosely and rejecting prestige and power. Their lives were characterized by prayer, contemplation, silence, solitude, attention to the Christian Scriptures, and concern and care for the poor.

Individuals

Throughout this time, there were certain people who made comments – comments that really made an impact and stuck with me.

At my grandparents' Baptist Church, the speaker quoted Mark 8:34:

> ...*deny yourself, take up your cross, and follow me.*

To paraphrase, "If people want to follow me, they must give up the things they want. They must be willing even to give up their lives to follow me." I was very familiar with this verse and the notion of self-denial, but the reality of it only dawned on my soul that day.

---

[19] You can read it online at
peacefulrivers.homestead.com/maryoliver.html

Though we intellectually understand and are familiar with the Biblical truths of sacrifice, surrender and self-denial, and whilst we are happy to read and sing about them, when it comes to putting them into practice it is an entirely different matter. In our narcissistic, self-absorbed culture where 'me time' is almost a right, we find Biblical truths like these unpalatable.

During early summer 2013, my closest childhood friend and I spoke about being "salt and light" in the world. The previous day had been a difficult one. I felt that my adultery had hardly been a "salt and light" decision, but it suddenly dawned on me that my decision to stay in my marriage was, and that hopefully this decision was bringing honour to God and to the name of Jesus in a sinful and cynical world. My friend's husband, my cousin, encouraged me that if I was making a definite choice then this demanded definite actions. I had been saying I wanted to stay in my marriage, but was still being pulled towards the other man.

During mid-summer 2013, at my home church, one of the deacons spoke of how, despite the culture we are in, despite the laws of this land, we are to remain faithful and obedient to the Word. He said that marriage, by God's definition, is lifelong, between one man and one woman, in the way that the church and Christ are one.

Again, I understood and had peace.

The very next week, again at my home church, another speaker spoke on Galatians 5 and said that for fruit to grow it needs good soil (like good fellowship, spending time in the Word and good choices). I suddenly understood that having made the right choice to stay in my marriage, I was living in the good of that right choice.

Once again, it all suddenly made sense and I moved a little closer to complete recovery.

One day, again in the early summer of 2013, a friend and I stood in the torrential rain in a wooded area near her home. There she spoke words of the Old Testament prophet Isaiah over me, personalizing the Scripture with my name. The passage can be found in Isaiah 40:1-2,5:

Comfort, comfort my [Esther]
Says your God.
Speak tenderly to [Esther]
And proclaim to her
That her hard service has been completed
That her sin has been paid for,
That she has received from the LORD's hand
Double for all her sins...
And the glory of the LORD will be revealed
And all people will see it together.
For the mouth of the LORD has spoken.

My friend anointed me with spikenard, just as David anointed himself after the death of his child, and she said, "Esther, know that you are cleansed from all your sins by the forgiveness Jesus purchased for you at the cross of Calvary. Go now and live your life as He has shown you, in the power of His Holy Spirit."

It was an incredibly powerful encounter with a friend I had only known for five weeks. Her connectivity, creativity and Holy Spirit energy never fail to bless me whenever I am in her company.

These encounters and profound moments were very special and I can only thank God for each of those individuals who were clearly being moved by the Holy

Spirit to speak these words, which in turn were being used to speak directly to me.

The dream

On January 21st, 2014, I had a dream – in fact two separate nightmares – in one night.

One depicted a little boy I had read about in a recent news article; he had been murdered by his mother and had been found on January 18th, 2014, buried in the field behind his aunt's house in Fife.

In my dream, he came to me as a very distressed adult carrying a stillborn baby. I told him he hadn't killed the baby; the baby was stillborn and I had the baby's birth certificate to prove it. I tried to reassure him that the dead baby was in heaven.

In my second dream, I was haemorrhaging in front of some work colleagues. I was mopping up the mess with a towel. No-one was helping me, just looking on. I didn't feel unwell at all and I wasn't afraid either.

I sent these dreams to be interpreted by 'Light & Life', and here is what one of the staff said in reply:

> ...there is much good, opportunity and favour to be found in your first dream. God is trying to reinforce something significant in your sphere of influence.
>
> The dream is about restoring balance and order. The boy's name means 'Who is like God?'
>
> The boy represents something or someone that is not in step with what God would do or

desires. God in heaven, however, has it under control.

In the second dream you are taking a large amount of responsibility or ownership for fixing a problem. It seems that the situation has not solely affected you but others are aware and you will be recognized for cleaning up any of the 'mess' that has occurred in this episode. You will find favour in this, and will serve as a good example to others even it if doesn't seem so at the time. Interestingly, Esther means 'star' and you have the opportunity to shine in this situation as you draw on wisdom from a deeper source.

I was quite speechless but extremely encouraged.

Psychology

I have a need to understand human nature – my own and others' – and by coming to an understanding, I usually find a further measure of peace.

I found a website (www.outofthefog.net) and was reminded that there were names given to the certain personality characteristics and disorders that I was struggling with – found in both myself and others. I read about obsessional love, the needy, the manipulative, the narcissistic personality and borderline personality disorder. Indeed, it literally is like coming "out of the fog" when there is some new-found knowledge gained and you begin to understand human behaviour more clearly.

I learned about the 51% rule, where we need to consider our own needs (in a relationship) just a little more than those of others.

The 50% rule states that we are responsible for 50% of the things that happen in any relationship.

I also learned about boundaries – healthy and unhealthy – and how to identify relationships in our lives which need a re-drawing of clear lines.

All of the psychology was immensely helpful to me and my foremost thought was, "I wish I had known all this twenty years ago."

Another thought that I found helpful was that a lot of these characteristics are present in all of us, should we care to admit it.

Attitude and Gratitude

During the summer of 2013, I was given 'One Thousand Gifts'[20] by Ann Voskamp to read. This was her list of one thousand things to be thankful for.

Having an attitude of thanksgiving and being mindful and grateful for my daily blessings has become something I have learned to do and continue to practice.

As Ann commented, learning requires practice:

I had never practiced [thankfulness] ... Practice is the hardest part of learning and training is the essence of transformation ... All

---

[20] Taken from *One Thousand Gifts* by Ann Voskamp. Copyright © 2011 by Ann Voskamp. Use by permission of Zondervan. *www.zondervan.com*

hard things come in due time and with practice.

She presented the ideas that...

Jesus offered thanksgiving for even that which broke him and crushed him and wounded him.

...and...

The act of sacrificing thank offerings to God – even for the bread and cup of cost, for cancer and crucifixion – this prepares the way for God to show us His fullest salvation from bitter, angry, resentful lives and from all sin that estranges us from Him.

Thanksgiving is the evidence of our acceptance of whatever He gives.

So, here is a small sample of the evidence of my gratitude to God, who continues to be at work in me:

LORD, I thank you for:

- the healing heat of the sun
- for love, mercy, grace and forgiveness
- for bees – don't let them be wiped out
- for tithing returned in surprising ways
- for bats that hoover up insects
- for a field of wild flowers and poppies
- for times of resting and reading
- for the salty smell of the sea and seaweed
- for pianos in unexpected places

- for ladybirds
- for laughter lines
- for family reunions
- for the heron who stalks the burn[21]
- for ferries
- for the sound of the harp
- for ancient yew trees
- for majestic birds of prey
- for the perspective of a child
- for thin places
- for waking up to worship songs in my head and for the way music reaches into places nothing else can
- for the white pheasant
- for scenery, silence, and solitude

Progress

I continue to be around family, pray, attend church, read my Bible and books and visit other thin places – places which are isolated and peaceful and good for the soul. I continue to listen to music and keep close accounts with a few good friends. Highs and lows still alternate (there are more highs than lows) but generally, stability has been achieved.

I still have invading thoughts and triggers (including, for example, driving certain stretches of the road, certain local street names, certain times of the year and writing this book) and these need to be managed. Generally, however, I am pleased to say that I have fully recovered,

---

[21] A little stream

perhaps to the extent that I am now my previous self plus a little bit more.

In sharing all of the personal insights described in this chapter, I feel as if my real self has been revealed. It is the miracle of redemption. I feel like I have been blind but now I can see.

CHAPTER SEVEN

The Desire of My Heart

Philippians 2:13
*God is working in you, giving you the desire
and the power to do what pleases Him.*

One of the ironies of faith is that despite our
weaknesses, we can still be used.[22]

The Lord used Samson's weakness, born of failure,
to enable him to do the mightiest work he had ever done.
His weakness was turned to strength.

It might not sit well with you (or even with me!) that
my slate has been wiped clean even after committing
adultery. This may reflect a lack of insight into the fact
that your slate needs to be wiped clean too. By being
forgiven, I can extend that same understanding towards
others, can relate to them and them to me, and I can live
humbly and non-judgmentally.

- I want this book to be used to reach out to others
  whose lives have been affected by adultery.

---

[22] See 2 Corinthians 12:10

- I want to expose my weaknesses so that others can also reveal theirs.
- I can live with the feeling of vulnerability if it means that others can be reached.
- I want to be real so that others can stop pretending.
- I want the devil to be defeated in the area of sexual sin, of any sort.
- I would love to see prodigals return.

To quote Psalm 51 (which David wrote after Nathan had confronted him about his adultery):

Psalm 51:12-13 (NIV)
Restore to me the joy of your salvation and grant me a willing spirit to sustain me. Then I will teach transgressors your ways, and sinners will turn back to you.

The desire of my heart is to see believers who have sinned turn back to Him, to turn back to believing and living the Scriptures wholeheartedly, and subsequently being spiritually transformed.

I believe the secret of this kind of life is to live as Jesus would have us live. What does that mean and what does He ask of us?

During late 2012, I wrote this in my prayer diary:

'Obedience' to the Word is my bottom line regardless of my feelings or my natural urges. Doing what is right matters.

The Word says to me 'marriage should be honoured by all'.

It encourages me to patiently endure, to live self sacrificially and to look after my husband to the end of his or my life as an act of service. (Note to self: People make sacrifices all the time for their children but they are somehow mystified if the sacrifice you make is for your marriage partner. This is not martyrdom but obedience.)

I believe God will honour my decision and will restore all of us involved.

The desire of my heart is to never commit adultery again in any shape or form;

- *to have no more lies and deceit in my life; and*

- *to be the best wife to my husband as I possibly can be from here on in till death do us part.*

As mentioned previously, we do not find the Biblical truths of self-denial, surrender, obedience, living sacrificially and serving others to be very palatable.

Whilst the Bible clearly teaches self-worth, it also denounces self-interest. When Jesus was asked what the greatest commandment was, He said that we were to love God with all our hearts, and love others with the same concern that we show for ourselves (Mark 12:30-31). When we obsess over ourselves, we lose the meaning of life, which is to love and serve God, and love and serve our neighbours. In a

2003 report, 'Hardwired to Connect', thirty-three research scientists discovered that we are biologically primed to find meaning through relationships. Chuck Colson said, 'After nearly eight decades of living, I can vouch for this. My single greatest joy is giving myself to others and seeing them grow in return. You cannot discover that without commitment. I first learned it by watching my parents care for my dying grandparents in our home and I later saw it in the Marine Corps. You cannot go into combat, commanding forty-five men as I was trained to do, if you weren't committed to one another. You were going to die if the man next to you did not cover your back. By abandoning commitment, our narcissistic culture has lost the one thing it desperately seeks: happiness. Without commitment, our individual lives will be barren and sterile. Without commitment, our lives will lack meaning and purpose. After all, if nothing is worth dying for, then nothing is worth living for. Jesus taught that the only way to live abundantly is to die to self-interest and give yourself fully to God, and to those who need what God has given you.'[23]

---

[23] United Christian Broadcast, Word For Today, March 10th 2014. UCB Operations Centre, Westport Road, Stoke on Trent, ST6 4JF. Free issues are available for the UK and Republic of Ireland. tel 0845-6040401 / e ucb@ucb.co.uk

We prefer to cling on to our bad habits, our sinful relationships and our idols (an idol being anything or anyone who has taken God's place in your life).

We sing:

> *Were the whole realm of nature mine,*
> *That were an offering far too small*
> *Love so amazing, so divine*
> *Demands my soul, my life, my all.*[24]

In this song, the lyrics show how we are called to give 100% to the Lord and nothing less. And yet, we are unwilling to let our bad habits, our sinful relationships and our idols go for fear of disintegrating and becoming empty. The irony is, when we do learn to let them go, we find peace, life and rest.

Far from disintegrating, we learn that in emptying, we become full and that to gain we have to lose; we only fall apart to be built back up again. In the end, we resemble more of how God intended us to be in the first place – we are broken to become more patient, more gentle, more kind, more Christ-like.

We have to renounce our will.

We are not our own – we have been bought with a price.

We are to be holy – set apart for Him, ready to do His will.

Salvation may be free but His amazing, divine love was immensely costly. Jesus died an agonizing death. He was abandoned so that we would not need to be.

He did that for me.

---

[24] *When I Survey the Wondrous Cross;* Isaac Watts (1707)

He did that for you.

How are you going to respond?

What are you going to do for Him?

Daniel 12:10 says that during the time of trial, many will be *"purified, cleansed and refined"*. I certainly feel that this has been true for me.

In our Western society we don't tend to suffer from lack of knowledge but we most certainly do suffer from lack of wisdom. Now the desire of my heart is to seek the serenity and the wisdom that He alone can give.

It all depends on the direction I am facing. If I am facing earth, human relationships take on the ultimate importance. If facing heaven, then my relationship with Jesus remains my first love and I aim to please Him (2 Cor. 5:9) and not myself.

I desire also to live each day flowing with the rhythm of life and, in doing so, offer my life as a living sacrifice back to Him.

I cannot offer him something that has cost me nothing.[25]

---

[25] See 2 Samuel 24:24

CHAPTER EIGHT

Concluding Thoughts

This book does not seek to comment on marriages that may be difficult, either because of being abusive, unhappy or because of an unequal yoke. Neither does it comment on divorce other than to say that divorce is permitted if one partner has committed adultery. I have also mentioned that if the non-believer wants to leave the believer, the Bible says the believer is not bound to that marriage.

This is simply my story. My hope is that it reaches and touches you, even if only in a small way.

If you are helping someone who is committing or has committed adultery, may I offer some words of advice?

- Have compassion.
- Speak the truth in love. This permission should not be used to condemn or judge. Simply show them what the Scripture says and leave the Holy Spirit to do the convicting.

Bob Gass commented:

Saying what needs to be heard is often hard, but, being a friend requires saying difficult things. Truth spoken in love can release people from their delusions, misperceptions, and inflexibility to live free, productive lives.[26]

- Listen to understand and not necessarily to reply.
- Don't judge progress based on time passing. Some say it can take one, two or even three years to recover from an experience like this and come to terms with what has happened. Some people don't have the ability to have the kind of patience required for the long haul. I remember on one occasion after ten months someone commenting that "we should get ourselves sorted out", and I remember thinking that I would not burden this person with my troubles again. And I never did.
- Some made suggestions like, "Let him go – just forget about him." In my experience this cannot be forced or be done by an act of the will. It simply occurs with the passage of time. For me, the emotional bond and the soul tie to the other man took about two years to be finally broken.

---

[26] United Christian Broadcast Daily Notes; October 28th 2013. UCB Operations Centre, Westport Road, Stoke on Trent, ST6 4JF. Free issues are available for the UK and Republic of Ireland. tel 0845-6040401 / e ucb@ucb.co.uk

- Suggest to them that they seek forgiveness from all the people that they have hurt. This includes forgiving themselves.

To prevent adultery becoming a serial offense:

- Learn to deal with the build-up of boredom, restlessness, disappointment and resentment within your marriage. A new relationship may relieve boredom but eventually this relationship will disappoint you, too. Learn to deal with the root cause or it will follow you around from relationship to relationship.
- Try an Alpha Marriage course.
- Involve the police if necessary to stop persistent unwanted communication, stalking or harassment.
- Learn to identify attraction at the earliest stage.
- Learn to say no to having coffees together, to becoming Facebook friends. Simply learn to say no, full-stop.
- Learn to protect your boundaries and put them into practice.
- Learn to block someone on Facebook.
- I would advise that those gifts which have been received by the lover should be removed from the marriage home. This may include gadgets, CDs, jewellery, watches or lingerie. Keeping them (especially in secret) perpetuates your double life and your divided loyalties. It also keeps you tied to objects that are reminders of the other person. Get rid of them even if it is a wrench. It is part of the final cleansing, the breaking of ties.

- Learn to identify where God may be challenging you about any area of your life where there is disobedience.

I end where I began.

Like Paul, we don't need to parade our failures or to pretend they didn't happen. Instead we thank the Lord that through His grace and power, our past is forgiven, our present is changed and our future is bright with hope for all that He has prepared for us.[27]

Psalm 119:7
I will thank you by living as I should.

---

[27] Our Daily Bread, Radio Bible Class, 13th October 2013; David McCasland

For Further Study

Old Testament

TEN COMMANDMENTS / MOSAIC LAW:

> **Deuteronomy 5:18**
> *Do not commit adultery.*

Read Leviticus 20:10, 18:25. In the letter of the law, those who committed adultery were to be stoned because they had been defiled and subsequently had defiled the land.

CONCERNING KING DAVID'S ADULTERY:

> **2 Samuel 11:4**
> *Then David sent messengers to get her; and when she came to the palace, he slept with her. She had just completed the purification rites after having her menstrual period. Then she returned home.*

KING DAVID'S RESPONSE TO HIS OWN SIN:

Read Psalm 51.

New Testament

COMMENTARY ON KING DAVID:

The New Testament describes King David, despite his adultery, as follows:

Acts 13:22
But God removed Saul and replaced him with David, a man about whom God said, 'I have found David son of Jesse, a man after my own heart...'

WARNINGS FROM ISRAEL'S HISTORY:

1 Corinthians 10:6,8
These things happened as a warning to us, so that we would not crave evil things as they did ... And we must not engage in sexual immorality as some of them did, causing 23,000 of them to die in one day.

OTHER INSTRUCTIONS:

1 Corinthians 6:18
Run from sexual sin! No other sin so clearly affects the body as this one does. For sexual immorality is a sin against your own body.

Hebrews 13:4
Give honour to marriage, and remain faithful to one another in marriage. God will surely judge people who are immoral and those who commit adultery.

Hebrews also describes those who choose not to confess their sin.

Hebrews 6:6
It is impossible to bring such people back to repentance; by rejecting the Son of God, they themselves are nailing him to the cross once again and holding him up to public shame.

John 8 tells the story of the woman caught in the act of adultery during Jesus' time.

Finally, warnings to sexually immoral believers are given in Revelation 2. Read the instructions to the churches in Pergamum and Thyatira.

The Formula

Combining David's story with that of the advice to the woman and the warnings to the churches, it appears obvious that to be made right again with God, the sinning believer should firstly admit their guilt, confess to others and to God, and finally repent and sin no more.

Supplementary Material

For additional comments and help, please visit the book's social media page, maintained by the author:

SCAN ME!

www.facebook.com/myfailureismyministry

or search on Facebook for 'Forsaking All Others'

Related Books from the Publisher

The Hidden Ministry
Muthoni

ISBN 978-1-910197-49-3

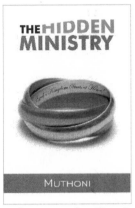

What is God's purpose for marriage and family life in the twenty-first century? Jesus calls the church his bride. So in some way our marriages are meant to point to God's eternal plan for every believer. Unpacking this, and drawing on Scripture, the author reveals keys to building strong family foundations, and shows how our 'hidden ministry' within our families is essential for a strong society and healthy churches.

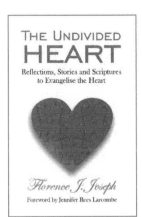

The Undivided Heart
Florence J. Joseph

ISBN 978-1-910197-30-1

Interspersed with humour, anecdotes, poems and stories, this book describes a journey of restoration, from its origins in God, through the broken and damaged places of our hearts, into the love of the Father and our place in His heart.